Zion-Benton Public Library District
Zion, Illinois 60099

DEMCO

Magic Johnson

PHOTO CREDITS
The National Basketball Association
Jon SooHoo: cover, pg. 6 and 25
Andrew Bernstein: pg. 2, 3, 10, 17, 29 and 30
Nathaniel Butler: pg. 13, 21
Ron Koch: pg. 9, 14, 18, 22 and 26

Distributed to Schools and Libraries
in Canada by
SAUNDERS BOOK COMPANY
Box 308
Collingwood, Ontario, Canada 69Y3Z7 / (800) 461-9120

Library of Congress Cataloging-in-Publication Data
Rothaus, James.
Magic Johnson / Jim Rothaus.
p. cm.
Summary: Describes the life and career of the basketball player
who earned his nickname "Magic" in high school
because of how well he handled the ball.
ISBN 0-89565-732-5
1. Johnson, Earvin, 1959-   —Juvenile literature.
2. Basketball players—United States—Biography—Juvenile literature.
3. Los Angeles Lakers (Basketball team)—Juvenile literature.
[1. Johnson, Earvin, 1959-   2. Basketball players.
3. Afro-Americans—Biography.] I. Title.
GV884.J63R68 1991   91-16394
796.323'092—dc20   CIP
[B]   AC

Magic Johnson

by James R. Rothaus

Earvin Johnson Jr.'s parents never had to wake him up for school in the morning. He was already up. And he was already at school. But little Earvin wasn't in the classroom yet. He was in the schoolyard, playing basketball. At 7:30 a.m. "People thought I was crazy," Johnson said. "They really, seriously did." Johnson wasn't crazy. He was doing what he loved. With a basketball in his hand, Earvin was in control. Even though he was one of the biggest kids in the schoolyard, Johnson played guard, not center.

Johnson grew up in Lansing, Michigan. He spent most of the time on the basketball court. By the time he got to high school, Earvin was already a local legend. At Everett High School, Johnson starred on one of the top teams in the state. He also had a flashy nickname. The coaches and players called him "Magic" because he could handle the ball so well. He had the size of a center, but the skills of a point guard.

 He was nicknamed "Magic."

Johnson liked his nickname. His mother, Christine, didn't
like it that much. "When you say
'Magic,' people expect so much,"
Christine Johnson said. "I was
afraid that it would give him a lot to
live up to at some point." Magic,
however, managed to live up to what
everybody expected from him. He
led Everett High School to the state
championship his senior year. Some
experts thought he was the best
high-school player in the country.

Johnson could have gone to any college in the country, but he chose to stay close to home. He went to nearby Michigan State University. As a freshman, he led Michigan State to the NCAA tournament. As a sophomore, he carried the team to the 1979 NCAA championship. In the championship game, Michigan State defeated Indiana State and its star, Larry Bird. Magic could have stayed in school for two more years. But he decided to turn pro. He was the first player picked in the 1979 National Basketball Association draft.

Magic was taken by the Los Angeles Lakers, a team led by superstar center Kareem Abdul-Jabbar. The Lakers were a good team, but not a championship team. Some experts believed Abdul-Jabbar had lost his love for the game. Magic brought a new attitude to the Lakers. That showed in the first NBA game Magic ever played. The Lakers were behind the San Diego Clippers by a point with seconds left.

Johnson got the ball to Kareem, who hit a long hook shot at the buzzer to win the game. Magic grabbed Kareem, and the two jumped around as if they had just won a championship. "At one point," said Denver coach Doug Moe, "I thought Kareem had had it with basketball. He loafed a lot. He plays harder now than he did before Magic was there." Some people were worried that having two stars on the team would cause problems. After all, this was Kareem's team, but everybody was talking about Magic.

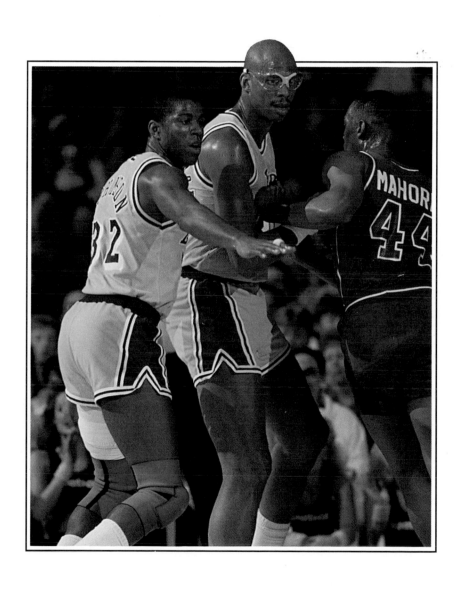

But Kareem was glad to
have Johnson around to run the
Laker offense. "All he wants to do
is get the ball to somebody else and
let them score," Abdul-Jabbar
explained. "If you're a big man,
it's not hard to like somebody like
that." Magic and Kareem led the
Lakers to the 1980 NBA championship series against the Philadelphia
76ers. Los Angeles took a three
games to two lead in the best-of-
seven series. But the Lakers had
to play the sixth game without
Abdul-Jabbar, who had a sprained
ankle.

The Lakers replaced Kareem with a new center. His name was Magic Johnson. All Johnson did was score forty-two points and grab eighteen rebounds in that sixth game. The Lakers won, giving them the NBA title. Magic had turned from playmaker into scorer just when Los Angeles needed it. That would become his trademark. Whatever the Lakers needed, he did. Playmaking? No problem. Scoring? If nobody else stepped forward. Rebounding? The six-foot-nine Magic did that as well as any guard in the league.

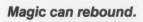

Other teams never knew what to expect from Johnson. But they did know that he would probably hurt them somehow. "The thing about Magic is that it's hard to tell if he's getting better, because he just does what he wants to do," said Portland guard Jim Paxson. "He can score only six points and totally dominate the game. Or he can decide they need points, and then go out and score thirty-nine. He just reads the flow of the game and decides what he's going to do that night."

Before each game, Johnson does the same thing. "I always listen to music," he said. "It gets me going, pumps my blood up. You get too uptight if you're thinking about the game all day." Magic sometimes likes to share his love of music with others. "I'll never forget walking through the airport with him," recalled Laker guard Norm Nixon. "He'd have his Walkman on. All of sudden, you'd hear somebody singing. There he'd be, stopped in the middle of the airport, singing his song and dancing with himself."

25

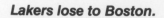

Lakers lose to Boston.

Unfortunately for Magic and the Lakers, the team would have troubles after the 1980 championship season. Los Angeles lost in the first round of the playoffs the next year. Many blamed Magic for the defeat. After winning the 1982 NBA title, the Lakers lost in the championship series in both 1983 and 1984. The loss in 1984 was to the Boston Celtics and Larry Bird. Magic again was blamed by some for the defeat. To some experts, the magic in Earvin Johnson's play had disappeared.

In 1985 Johnson took the court with a new attitude. No more fun and games. He was there to win championships. "If you notice," said his mother, "before when he was playing he used to smile a lot. But now he doesn't smile as much. It's just a sign of his new determination." Magic and Kareem led the Lakers to the NBA championship in 1985. Two years later, Johnson put together his best season. He was named NBA Most Valuable Player for the first time. He was also MVP of the playoffs, as Los Angeles defeated Bird and Boston in the 1987 championship series.

Magic is an MVP.

The Lakers won the league title again in 1988. They became the first team in nineteen years to win back-to-back NBA championships. It was the fifth time Los Angeles had won the league title in Johnson's nine years in the NBA. No player in the league had a greater impact during the 1980s than Magic Johnson. But then, Earvin Johnson, Jr. has been a winner since he was a young kid in the schoolyard. All those mornings of getting up to play basketball have paid off. "Magic" has lived up to his nickname.